EXTREME ANIMALS

CRAZY CREEPY CRAWLIES

Isabel Thomas

Raintree

Chicago, Illinois

www.capstonepub.com
Visit our website to find out more information about Heinemann-Raintree books.

To order:

☎ Phone 800-747-4992

🖥 Visit www.capstonepub.com to browse our catalog and order online.

© 2013 Raintree
an imprint of Capstone Global Library, LLC
Chicago, Illinois

Edited by Daniel Nunn, John-Paul Wilkins, and Rebecca Rissman
Designed by Philippa Jenkins
Picture research by Elizabeth Alexander
Production by Victoria Fitzgerald

Originated by Capstone Global Library
Printed and bound in China by CTPS

16 15 14 13 12
10 9 8 7 6 5 4 3 2 1

Library of Congress Cataloging-in-Publication Data

Cataloging-in-Publication data is on file at the Library of Congress.

ISBN:

978-1-4109-4679-9 (HC) 978-1-4109-4685-0 (PB)

Acknowledgments

We would like to thank the following for permission to reproduce photographs: Alamy pp. 6 (© mauritius images GmbH), 11 (© Image Quest Marine), 13 (© Whitehead Images); Ardea.com p. 25 (© Auscape); Corbis p. 23 (© Frans Lanting); Dreamstime.com p. 26 (© Ryszard); FLPA pp. 18, 19 (Mark Moffett/Minden Pictures); Getty Images pp. 4 (Roger de la Harpe/Gallo Images), 12 (Frank Greenaway/Dorling Kindersley); Nature Picture Library p. 21 (© Doug Wechsler); NHPA pp. 14 (Daniel Heuclin), 15 (© Stephen Dalton), 27 (George Bernard); Photolibrary pp. 5, 16 (Satoshi Kuribayashi/OSF), 10 (Carlos Martínez/Age fotostock), 17 (John Mitchell/OSF), 22 (Gavriel Jecan/Age fotostock); Shutterstock pp. 7 (© Nick Stubbs), 8 (© Fong Kam Yee), 9 (© Horia Bogdan), 20 (© Smit), 24 (© EcoPrint).

Main cover photograph of a giant Asian mantis eating a cricket reproduced with permission of Shutterstock (© Cathy Keifer). Background cover photograph reproduced with permission of Shutterstock (© EW CHEE GUAN).

Some words are shown in bold, **like this**. You can find out what they mean by looking in the glossary.

Contents

Extreme Creepy Crawlies

Do you think you know everything about creepy crawlies? Think again! All creepy crawlies have hard outer bodies with squishy insides. But the differences between them are what make them **extreme**.

thick-tailed scorpion

This Bombardier beetle has an extreme way to scare predators. It sprays boiling poison from its bottom!

Strange features or behavior help creepy crawlies to find **mates** or food—or to not get eaten themselves!

Beastly Beetles

Visit almost any land **habitat**, and you will find a beetle living there. There are more types of beetle than any other insect in the world. They come in many different shapes and sizes.

This Namib Desert beetle can catch water from fog on it's wings. This helps the beetle to live in very dry places.

dung

DID YOU KNOW?
Dung beetles feed on animal droppings!

7

If there were a bug Olympics, beetles would be the stars. Australian tiger beetles are the world's fastest-running insects. If they were human-sized, they would be able to beat a race car going at top speed!

Imagine if you could lift 17 cars. A rhinoceros beetle could if it were your size. They can lift things 850 times heavier than themselves.

horn for fighting other beetles

Masters of Disguise

Mantises have amazing **camouflage**. The shapes and colors of their bodies match their **habitat**. This helps them to **ambush** their **prey**. Their big, spiny front legs are used to grab prey and stop it from getting away.

leaf-colored wings

sharp spines

prey

DID YOU KNOW?

The orchid mantis looks just like an orchid flower!
Can you spot it?

Don't Eat Me!

Bugs may be snack-sized, but they do not want to be eaten. Centipedes and millipedes have some **extreme** ways to scare off **predators**. Millipedes squirt out poisonous chemicals when they are in danger.

centipede

This giant centipede's bright colors are a warning: "Don't try to eat me, I have poisonous fangs!"

The shocking pink dragon millepede from Thailand is just 1 inch long. Its bright color is a warning to predators to stay away.

Super-Strong Silk

Spider silk is stronger than steel and tougher than a bulletproof vest! It is perfect for trapping fast-moving **prey**. In the Solomon Islands, near Australia, people use the big webs of orb-web spiders as fishing nets.

bird caught in web

orb-web spider

DID YOU KNOW?

Baby spiders can fly using their silk. The wind can carry them thousands of miles!

Jumping spiders do not need webs. They can leap 50 times their own length. This is like a 100-yard sprinter leaping from the start to the finish line! The spiders' huge eyes help them land right on top of their **prey**.

The Goliath tarantula is the world's heaviest spider. It has even been known to eat birds!

The tarantula hawk wasp is a tarantula's worst nightmare! The wasp **paralyzes** the tarantula with a sting so that it cannot move. Then it drags it to its burrow and lays an egg on it. When the egg hatches, the wasp **larva** eats the tarantula alive!

burrow

tarantula

wasp larva

19

Tiny but Noisy

Cicadas are the world's loudest insects. They **vibrate** little drum-like parts on their bodies to make a noise louder than thunder or trains!

noise-making drum

Some cicadas spend their first 17 years underground. Hundreds of thousands of cicadas come to the surface at the same time to **mate**. They die after just two weeks.

Migrating Monarchs

Imagine the chaos if everyone in Mexico decided to go on vacation to Canada at the same time! Every year, 100 million Monarch butterflies make this journey together. They **migrate** up to an incredible 2,800 miles!

Birds and other **predators** leave the butterflies alone. Baby butterflies eat milkweed, which makes them poisonous as adults.

Terrifying Teamwork

Termites live in **colonies** of millions or billions. They are tiny, but they work together to build enormous homes. Their mounds can be taller than a giraffe. They are made of earth, spit, and **dung**!

termite mound

DID YOU KNOW?

Australian termites munch through everything from wood and tires to electric cables. They destroy houses and bridges.

Army ants are fearsome **predators**.
They work in teams to attack much
bigger animals. They swarm over
anything in their path. They bite and
sting their **prey** to death.

DID YOU KNOW?

The only way to escape army ants is to stay totally still. Army ants are blind. They can only find prey that is moving or making a noise.

Record-Breakers

Which creepy crawly do you think is the most **extreme**? Why? Take a look at some of these record-breaking creepy crawlies to help you decide.

What? Giant huntsman spider

Why? World's largest spider

Wow! These megabeasts have a leg span of 12 inches. That is as long as a classroom ruler!

What? Australian tiger beetle

Why? Fastest-running insect

Wow! This super sprinter can travel 8 feet every second when chasing **prey**.

What? Goliath tarantula

Why? Longest fangs

Wow! These spiders have fangs up to half an inch long. Their bite is painful, but it is not dangerous for humans.

What? Goliath beetle

Why? World's heaviest insect

Wow! They can weigh as much as a large apple.

What? Millipede

Why? Most legs

Wow! A Californian millipede holds the record for the most legs, with 375 pairs, or 750 legs!

What? Fairy fly

Why? World's smallest insect

Wow! The smallest males measure just 0.007 of an inch. You could fit five of them on a period on this page!

ambush attack an animal from a hiding place

camouflage colors or markings that help an animal to blend in with the things around it

colony group of many animals of one kind that live together

dung animal droppings

extreme unusual, amazing, or different from normal

habitat natural home of an animal

larva insect in its first stage after hatching from an egg

mate come together to produce young. An animal's mate is the male or female it mates with.

migrate move from one place to another when the seasons change

paralyze take away the ability to move

predator animal that hunts other animals for food

prey animal that is hunted by another animal for food

vibrate cause something to make small back-and-forth movements that make a noise

Find Out More

Books

Johnson, Jinny. *Insects and Creepy-Crawlies* (Explorers). New York: Kingfisher, 2011.

O'Neill, Amanda. *I Wonder Why Spiders Spin Webs and Other Questions About Creepy-Crawlies* (I Wonder Why). New York: Kingfisher, 2011.

Solway, Andrew. *Deadly Insects* (Wild Predators). Chicago: Heinemann Library, 2005.

Web sites

Watch videos of creepy crawlies and animals at this National Geographic web site:
animals.nationalgeographic.com/animals/bugs/

Learn more about all kinds of insects at this web site of the San Diego Zoo:
kids.sandiegozoo.org/animals/insects

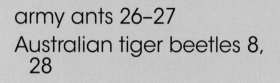